Lost In It
With Nowhere
To Run

Brandon Ogle

LOST IN IT WITH NOWHERE TO RUN Copyright © 2015 Brandon Ogle. Printed and bound in the United States of America. All rights reserved. No part of this book may be reproduced or transmitted in any form or by any means, electronic or mechanical, including photocopying, recording, or by an information storage and retrieval system—except by a reviewer who may quote brief passages in a review to be printed in a magazine, newspaper, or on the Web—without written permission from the publisher.

ISBN 978-0-578-17020-6

Madness dwells in the heart
Driving mad those doomed
To wander its sundrenched shores

Preface

Love is a vicious cycle that no one can escape. In the beginning as we learn how it all works, the cycles trample us in a flash it seems. As we stumble to our feet from the lesson each one teaches us the footing becomes more secure. Every cycle endured appears to be enhanced and easier to maintain, slowing with each pass. Stretching out beyond the months that become years, imparting the great joys and damaging disappointments that make up our lives. When the great one comes we feel it in our bones, committing completely to fighting tooth and nail for every second with the love of our lives. Dreams of Winnebago freedom, rocking chair porches or ocean side balconies soaked in pinot grigio colonize the minds of lovers picturing twilight years of bliss.

What follows is my own experience and articulation of some of love's cycles that found me caught in the middle of stampedes. Fleeting and as quickly passing as they were lessons were learned, character was built and the foundation was laid for this boy to grow upon. None were the love of my life (although otherwise stated within the haze of love's blinding ways) for that was found much later. There is no balcony, the ocean is a little farther away but within reach and the pinot has been traded for bourbon. It is perfect. The thing dreams are made of and love envies. This cycle has nearly paused for me, and at the best part of my movie.

Please enjoy the ramblings from this madman's pen and know that lines may blur and words may falter, but love is never ending. Even in its most painful throws of protest. Let these pages cover you with the memories of emotional states that froze you in time and had you cherishing every minute.

camel skeleton	5
wonderful torture	6
pool of therapy	10
chaotic silence	11
soft liquid	13
necessary world	14
staring out a window	15
boxed in	16
menial things	17
smoke to forget	19
wilting	21
stone or pill	22
pathetic deeds	23
dancing mad and fine	24
a long way from everything	25
always lying	26
veil of confusion	27
blankly wandering	28
fleeting masses	29
a lovely man	31
first plunge	32
should you	33
cabinet	34
darkened path	35
forward movement	36
high stakes	37
dark red hair	38
faint whispers	40
the ink bleeds	42
waxy vision	43
naked vixen	44
insecurities disappear	45

ninety-nine ways	46
naked and on trial	47
saved	49
devil's slumber	50
disturbing portrayal	51
a night at the circus	52
whispered rumors	53
empty hook	55
laughing solemnly	56
shoulder of evil	57
fire rises	58
gorge yourself	59
for sam	61
shimmering life	64
the sad mask	65
pendulum	66
rays of hope	68
floating death	69
rubble	70
smoke filled vacation	71
genesis	72
voids of eternity	73
dream state	74
destruction	75
misty eyed	76
predestined	77
living memories	78
small boy	79
highway solitude	80
closed eyes	81
convincing yourself	82
lost freaks	83

young warrior	84
soft journey	85
hypnotized	86
desolate	87
stained hands of hate	89
struggle continues	90
face of divine will	91
other times there is too little	93
lost in slumber	94
how you played	95
sheeted world	96
blurry haze	98
strangers	99
lost in it	100
blind or crazy	101
despised feelings	102
prince in keeping	104
2:50	105
porcelain god	106
days pass	107
otherworldly	108
secrets	109
moving to the beat	110
chance meeting	111
the jockey	113
shake me	114
dirty window	115
lament the lovers	116
unfitting symbol	117
jealousy	118
car	119
miscommunications	121

me, myself and i	123
lovely day out	124
eighteen years of sadness	125
speeding through the rain	126
old faces new times	127
new nation	128
pickle	129
apostles and profits	130
navigation	131
god's tears	132
further down the road	133
lonely souls	134
lost simple ways	135
patriot	136
greasing the wheel	138
uncertain parenthood	139
midnight hour	141
blonde savior	142
nonchalant-ness	143
corner seat	144
in the clouds	145
keep pouring the salt in	146
be happy	147
buzzard	148
rough man	149
ego overdose	150
not a career	151
constant mask	160
regenerative nature of souls	161
hot ash	162
succumb to exploiting	164
insensitive cold	166

unchained whispers	167
perfect shells	169
eye of the beholder	170
muddied transgressions	172
white knight	174
arduous wait	175
life's nectar	177
keeper of the flame	179
reassuring hand	181
bumpy ride	182
other side of morning	183
trivial distance	184
positive outlook of the future	185
escape it all	187
tedious moments	189
4:42 am	190
she's finally here	192
toxic disregard	193
other's words	194

**Lost In It
With Nowhere
To Run**

Total disregard for the loose description of humanity
That we place upon those that walk around us
Slowly disintegrating the moral fiber
Holding close what we once
Let go of so easily

camel skeleton

An empty convenience store coffee container sits by me on the coffee table.
The select blend inside now warming my stomach.
The skeleton of a Camel perches at ehe far end,
Smoked earlier in the day now just sitting there holding the last of itself together in feathery ash reminding you of her.
The way she clutched onto the simple cord you gave to her on that night after Hallmark's love money making holiday.
So simple a gesture.

Others notice now.
The playful little pats and tickles that pass between the two of us.
The longings for something that was lost or maybe put on hold to converse with another voice that waits patiently on the other line.
Switching the attention to a new flame.

Light shines from many strange places.
Looking to your face as a guide through this dark desolate world you left me in.
Seems ironic as hell.
Not my depending on you,
Just the thought of needing you so much to get by.

My stone sets in and it ends up slipping away and running back,
Like children teasing their peers.
Here it is take it.
But don't think you can have it.
It's not for you
Not right now.

wonderful torture

Things unfold in time and you're impatient as hell.
Everything should be now,
It should all fall right into place and be waiting like a car waits to be driven.
Smoking dope and thinking everything's fine.
She's beside you on the bed playing with what's left of your mind.
Is there as a friend,
Or a lonely lover from your past wanting to join you again bringing wonderful torture that you've missed.
Nothing escapes either mouth as to which way it will fall,
Or if it ever will.
Just guesses as to how long you can last and what might come to you afterwards.
There you sit with such lovely confusion,
And friendship surrounding you feeling spectacular.
Then you realize that you're probably just stoned.

broken windows

Every word you write
Sends you spiraling downward.
You tell yourself the
Next line will have
Nothing to do with her
And yet every word
Relates back to her,
She's in you,
Killing everything inside
Of you and laughing.
Evil grins shoot from her mouth
Tearing into you as you.
Catch small elegant glances that hold
Stories of novel length and poems that ring with love forever.

This ghost that haunts your page, dreams and life was asked for,
Remember?
You called upon its powers and now dealing with them is unbearable.
Sometimes the most evil of hells is asked for.

Struggling the turtle remains on its back until death,
And erupting from its sun-bleached bones stands a dove as beautiful
as the day you started to walk down the paths of Heaven with her by
your side.
Questions fly through broken windows of thought never coming
across a complete answer,
Dying in midflight.

black wax

Hard to see the light
From the candle that
Slowly dripped black wax
On your heart that's
Now been stifled.
Sparks appear to fly
From the charred wick,
You realize it's
Just hope and settle
Back into the seat
That's molded around
Your ass from the
Long hours of anguish
You've endured in it.
The wax is still
Warm somehow.
Almost sticky to
The touch of your
Fingertips as you
Dream the same
Dreams over and
Over again in your mind.
The dreams of that
Small candle and its
Light that you helped evoke.
Funny how things
Take on a new
Appearance after they've
Been burned by
Uncontrollable fires
That can only be
Started in the bowels
Of a rotting heart.

You sit there
(Blackened by flames
That had to have
An invitation to
Grace you with their
Destructively beautiful presence)
Wondering how you could
Beckon them back.
Remembering the burn
You felt when engulfed
By the arms of the
Red lover and the
Scent it left behind
To torture you with.
Remembering everything
About it and wanting it
There with you now.
Looking to the candle.
Sharing its pain.

pool of therapy

Thinking over a cup of black coffee.
Cigarette butts in the ashtray a small escape from a menial existence that now spills into this cup as a therapeutic act that has to be played out night after night,
If anything is to go on as quote unquote normal.
Looking down into the cup before you and everything that has spilled into it leaves nothing but her.
She's there swimming in the pool of therapy,
Catching your feelings as you drink to the memories.
Drinking to her.

chaotic silence

Still the silence hovers over.
Trapped in this chaotic
World where noise flies
As fast as the new
Temptations that try to
Distract you from her memory.
The silence is still
Encompassing you,
Keeping you locked to
Her elegant song
Screaming all the while.
Words you write
Run nowhere and
Travel to distant hearts
Full of your heaven.
Thoughts of death
Accompany her dance,
Matching every move
With psychotic precession.

Following pretty roads
North the soldier rode,
Laughing with intent bliss.
Maidens' screams filling
His head and thoughts
Of a queen whom he serves.

Taunting you with the
Most wonderful things
In all creation.
Laying yet more choices
To your already
Exhausted mind.

Humming tones and
Muffled voices strain
For your attention and
The one that holds it
Isn't even present.
Dreams run through your
Mind trampling as many
Thoughts as they can
To redeem you.
Tickling his senses,
Deadened and riding with
Death he giggles
Knowing it awaits yet
Needing the pleasure
The queen gives.
Death sleeps with
Angels,
Quenched and resting.

soft liquid

Soft liquid covers
Your bone-dry body
As of course she
Reenters your consciousness.
The warmth is welcomed
And frightening.
So long it's been
Since your body
Tightened with fear
While pleasant hopes
Linger on your memories.
Clear water beckons you.
Icy cool and sitting there,
Waiting for you to need it
Much like the wait
For you of her.
Promises mean nothing
To inanimate objects
So you keep giving
Them to everything
You own.
Hoping someday that it
Will crush her memory,
Freeing the demon
That wishes to devour
Your soul.
Giving it to someone
And left to deal
With the promises.

necessary world

Walking into the sad world.
A world created by necessity.
Something that gets you by,
Pays the rent,
Puts coffee in your gullet,
And keeps you high.
Looking at it all as a life
Starting blocks that are crumbling.
Shifty foundations bare beautiful children
And your life is unwanted.
Numbers stare you down
As slowly you start to give in.
Caving into her melodic pull you daze
Letting the line run with insane rings.
Voices cloud your head bringing you out.
Franticly calm you hang up
Scratch the number off and forget,
Walk around your hell
Try to forget the worry.
Concentrate on the reason for it all
Only to look forward to more
Of it tomorrow and the day after.
Money seems to comfort you for a few moments.
Reminds you of weekend dreams
That got you through school.
She's good but not enough.
Money fills the voids
Trying to make it all okay,
Needing her for use of it.

staring out a window

Staring out a window that knows you well.
Seeing the stifled cross
Wondering if it will light again.
Wanting to watch the simple ones
Searching for enjoyment on this eve.
The cross is out so no one comes.
Trapped in their homes with nothing,
Just memories.
The reflections taunt you with wavy images.
You watch as they eat
See them glance at you and wonder.
Gleaming hope, anticipation and loss
Wanting to live as you
Share what you have:
Nothing.
Their fading days pass quickly by.
Pain is a variable unwanted.
Lies in notches made by hands
That hold no master.
Floating near those with nothing
Maybe stealing a little to examine.
She frightens them and she's yours.
A therapeutic dose of heaven
To melt away the hell.

boxed in

Everything squares away a box
One you've created and can't destroy.
Destruction of beautiful things
Should be unlawful.
Punishable only by death and its rangers
Wearing shiny badges of pain
Gleaming in darkness's shadow
Lighting paths that lead nowhere.
Boxed away like a prisoner of your
Own fragile world.
Determined and distraught you think.
Think of lowly things that might
Heighten your senses.
Smoke a cigarette and relax in her,
Lie to her piercing eyes then smile
Knowing that she sees through it.
Knowing she feels your need and
Spits on it,
Discards it like the fleeting
Happiness you shared on bitter cold
Nights of love play.
Never really serious
Just created enough to fill the box.

menial things

Smoke clouds your mind
As you realize that's her
Favorite place to hide.
To wait for an unsuspecting heart
To wander along so that she
Might turn it to food
And devour it.
Hazy vision leaves her skewed,
Makes you wonder whether or
Not you ever saw her
Clearly to begin with.

Life can be wasted on many
Menial things
A heart is not among them.

Lovers taunt themselves with dreams,
Goals so high they fall short
And run from failure's glare.
You chase your thoughts with
An evil action and everything
Seems to be looking fine.
Mirrors aid magicians in their art.
They only show you what
She doesn't want.

Playing in the sandbox the child asks,
"What is it that makes people crazy?".
Shocked at the maturity you
Answer as best a crazy person can,
"Love my child, only love can
Drive one mad without knowledge of
The event taking place.".

Satisfied it returns to play.

Nothing can stop her from
Plundering your thoughts
So you start to give up.
Knowing that fighting it
Will only kill you and
A soldier's death is not
What you find appealing.
Slowly slipping away you
Kiss her memory and
Travel on to meet the child.

smoke to forget

Smoke to forget.
Destroy enough of
Yourself to ensure safety,
Leave nothing capable
Of feeling.
Then maybe the sun
Will open and blind
Your eyes to prevent
Their wandering ways.
Not away from her.
Dreams are made of
That feat,
The feat she holds.
Your willingness to care.
The love you saved
For someone worthy
And you gave it to her.
Idiocy prevails when
Blinded by beauty and
The perfect being
That rested in her.
Your stone keeps
You sane,
Without it she fills
Your every free
Moment of thought.
Under the delightful
Haze she seems to
Come less often.
You fight the feelings
And yet don't want
Them to die,
Much like the

Lost weeks spent
In utter bliss.
Treasures are found
With you staring the
Hunter in the face.
Lost cities are your home
And secrets run through
Your veins, licking the
Inside walls of heaven
Just to let them
Know the angel has
Returned.

wilting

It surrounds me.
Takes me to another plane.

You look to a flower
For some form of
Emotional support.
Wilting before you it sits,
Mocking the tears
That well but never fall.
Evil fills the day
And finally her memory fades.

My eyes are barely open.
Slipping into that eighth
Dimension in which
I can escape all thought,
Ponder everything that
Has nothing to do with
Her only to come up with
One thing.
Another hit comes my
Way and I forget
What it was I searched
So long for.
The only thing that doesn't
Remind me of her,
So there's nothing.
No escape.

stone or pill

Always in this now.
Trapped in a cycle
Of stone or pill.
Hide it with a false
Front of hazy eyes
Or unexplainable neurotic
Babbling from the
Speed hurricane until
They kick in and
Cause a calm still
Leaving thoughts to
Wander and pitch tents
On nerves you try
To deaden with toxic
Mixtures
One day success will
Come and surprise
You with a visit
Accompanied by death
There you can
Ponder it all
Peacefully.

pathetic deeds

Look at the feeble
Things you try.
Put thought to action,
Ponder what the hell
Is going on sometime.
Look at the fucking
Pathetic deeds you do
To win something
That doesn't even
Want your poor
No direction ass
Anyway, so that you
Can say hey
Look I'm really
Fucking happy!
Look at me I'm
So damn happy!
Finally I've found
The one for me.
Look she doesn't
Want me but she's
Still here trapped
With me and I'm really fucking happy!
Sure you can try to
Look at someone else,
Think about how you could
Lay all your problems
Down with them
So that you might
Someday move on.
But then what.

dancing mad and fine

All around you dancing mad and fine
Screaming, chanting, yelling to it from nowhere
Such a release and no one hears it
Out in the forbidden land of old
No returning now to what you once had
This is it
Your new home
Everything you own is now finally your own
Everything you think is now your own thought
Haunting things run beside you
And dance with the many things around
Let all of it go in smoke
Breath it and feel it burn
Watch it float in the room
Clouds of thought slowly sucked away
Through cracks you didn't know existed
Funny how thoughts linger there
Let you watch them, study them
Things like to be watched
They like to have the attention
They eat it up like savage warriors
Show you your heart before they lick your brain
Yes it sure is funny how thoughts linger there
Show it your pain and watch as it takes it
Feeds on it and takes it away as nothing
No problem for it so you study

Angels glance at you through tracers
Kiss you softly and scream in pain
They love you and need you dead.

a long way from everything

To get in the car and drive
Is all you wish to do now.
No destination in mind,
Anywhere but near it all.
Somewhere a long way from
Everything you've created here.
Leave it all behind you.
To see reflections of it
In your rearview and
Laugh as you smoke
The first cigarette in
The start of your new life.
This new adventure you
Started so that you
Can someday fuck this
One up as well.

always lying

Always lying there asking
Him for help.
Promising that you'll do
As much as you can if
He'll just pick up the rest.
Now look where you're at.
You showed a little
Initiative in the dilemma
And you're bombarded
With possibilities.
Did it actually come
Through as a freak glitch
This time or did
He see that you were
Actually trying and
Decided to help out.
Either way you're in deep.
Live the way the
Lizard does.
Fade away in your
Surroundings and let them
Work themselves out,
Or to death.

veil of confusion

Now you think of what it would be like
Sitting there across from another.

Wonder if she might find her way
Back into your mind right then
Ruining all of it with her memories.

Could anything keep her away,
Fend off her lovely evil.

She's always there with you,
Tormenting your thoughts and
Torturing your initiative to look
Search for another to share with.

You realize that you're damaged goods.

Everyone sees through the holy
Veil of confusion and smoke
That you've pulled down over you.

Lonely are the ones with memories
So you decide to destroy them
And at the same time end up
Destroying yourself.

blankly wandering

Blankly wandering into
Fear covering all so you step back.
Waiting is killing everything.
Plants without sunshine wilt and
Life is too short to waste
On this infantile uncertainty.
Courage rest in the souls of
Dead soldiers that fought
The battles that shaped
Your life so sickly now.
Wasted on this shell.
Emptiness so vast and
Immense your feelings fall
Through it and in to a hell
Having nothing to do now.
Torturing and self-destruction
Pass the time and the
Uselessness you now feel.
Keep a distance from your thoughts.
Let the carelessness of life
Take your will.

fleeting masses

Caves offer so much
Tranquility in this world.
Entering them strikes fear
In the souls of
Those who hold none.
The empty loss of the
Fleeting masses that stare
At you through the
Fogged over windows
To your soul,
Glazed over with the
Medication you've discovered
From your past.
Captured there in the
Mist that surrounds,
Voices call to you.
Try to save you from the dull.
The television remains as the
Source of your verbal torment.
On through the static
You hear them,
Their conversations become yours.
You're there with them
In the room they occupy.
A part of the movie
Taping it all in your head,
Manipulating the outcome,
Saving the chosen and destroying yourself.
Slowly wasting away in the mirror.
A skeleton is all that's there
Staring at you through the
Foggy steam that rises from your
Shower as if you were there

In the field predestined
For your death.
All mapped out for you,
So easy to follow and yet
You can't figure it all out.

a lovely man

A lovely man approached you today.
He asked you if you've ever
Been in love before and your answer
Brings laughter emptying from his being.
Every chuckle cut you,
Explaining it was a long time ago
Produces yet more laughter.
You begin to think what he
Tells you is true,
That you're trapped in it forever.
She'll always be there.
As he hobbled on past you wished
What he said wasn't true,
Knowing it was the only truth
You had heard in years.

first plunge

Already being told it's
The biggest mistake yet
And still you took
That first plunge and
Quickly lost your balance

So there you are
Wanting to go for it
But not knowing what it is

He wants to go

To maybe save you

Problem is you don't
Think you want to be

should you

You hope it's not something
Special with her,
Almost fear it.
Going back to the
Days of no feeling
Is the only thing
That can save you now.
Or so you think.
Either way you're in
Deep shit and there's
No way out.
Should you even try?
Should you even care?
You do have to see
Her everyday of your
Marketing career.
To piss off a fixture
In your life is not
A good thing,
Certain death in
Some fields.
Still for some thoughtless
Logicless mess of a
Reason you want it,
And all the shit that
Comes with it.

cabinet

It all subsides when you're stoned.
Doesn't really go away
You can just think about it
More openly and in greater intricacy.
Tear it down into the things
It offers and the things you want,
Then just pick what it is.
Files of things you can flip through.
File after file with your
Mental fingers throwing all of the
Things that would ruin happiness
Into a pile and all of the
Pieces that fit in another.
If the piles scale go for it,
Forget what all of the
Other people that keep
Whispering "mistake" say and do it.
You want it.
It's there.
Take it.
No one can flip through mental files
But you and only you care.
Most everything will fit together.
The ink they leave behind
Forming a mass picture within
Picture mind-scape that may
Turn out to be shit or
Beautiful as hell.
Chances are taken by those
Who wish to gain things,
And right now you have
Nothing to lose.

darkened path

Lost in a cold oblivion
And wondering if it
Lasts as long as the
Lovely glances you threw
Or much longer

Trapping this boy
Struggling to become a
Man and faced with the
Beauty you hold there
In front of him

There are always lit
Paths through the
Wooded parts of your
Life and still you
Choose the darkened ones

forward movement

It's been so long
Since we've been
Together in love.
Moving on seemed
Like the most
Sensible thing to
Do next.
Thought and action
Have and will always be
Two separate things.
Getting intimate with
Her kills me.
Thoughts of you
Rush over me and
Suddenly I'm cheating on you.
Nothing backs it up,
We're not even together.
Still I feel like I'm
Cheating on you!
Like I still belong
To you and only you.
Her kisses fall short
Of anything we ever
Shared and our bodies
Are pieces from different
Puzzles when we fit
Together perfectly.
Satisfaction will never
Approach this life.

high stakes

As the words leave your mouth
You wonder what you will say.
Nothing was planned out
You just grabbed for the phone.
Blowing it off would be easy.
Is anything ever going to
Solve this one problem,
Or will it stay with you forever.
So many times you've gone
Over what to say and
Now you can't remember
A word of it.
This situation is the most
Dangerous you've ever
Encountered and the
Stakes are too high to gamble with.
Folding would be your best bet,
But up until now that
Has only left you empty handed.

All you wish is to
Have her, or just
Not care about her.

dark red hair

The dark red hair
You caressed
Now haunts you.
Covers what you want most,
Her needs.

Puzzles that lend nothing,
Show no picture and
Have no meaning
Mean everything.

Drilling through fertile
Soils to reach the
Nutrients that feed
Your growing passion,
Only coming across
Boulders of confusion
That hinder your progress.
Little riddles that
Bleed your thoughts,
Distract you from the
Goal at hand.

Golden words float
Ahead of the bow.
Scrambled mixture of
Feeling, thought, anguish.
Insanity is a splendid
Thing that opens
Worlds of new experiences
And tells you the tales
Of their afterlives.

The freckled chest of
Your dove rests,
Slowly moving up and down
Then repeating.
As you watch her sleep
You realize how much
Love lies in your heart
For her.
Laughing to yourself softly.
She's the only thing
That's ever mattered
In your life.
Only thing you've ever
Put all of your heart into.
Fear of loss, jealousy,
These things never
Cross your mind
While thoughts of her linger.
Amazing how peaceful you
Feel with her.
Like children in their
Mother's arms.
She is your sanctuary.

faint whispers

Faint whispers echo
From nowhere
Letting you know
Exactly what you're
Heading for.

Nothing accompanies
Them with its wisdom
And lack of feeling,
Diagraming your every
Move to ensure complete
Unhappiness for you.

The only words you
Wish to speak
She can't hear.
Slowly you wilt
As the realization
Of what the two
Need means nothing
To anyone but the
Battered soul that
Hides in your mind.
Fighting the masked
Feelings weakens you.
Delusionary thoughts
That maybe she's
Fighting the same
Battle maddens you.
The dreams set in.

There she is yours
And the words flow

Freely as tears stain
The hands that once
Held her close.
Knowing that love
Welcomes no other
In your heart
As your lips touch.
Here it is real.
Her eyes lead nowhere
Important and it's
The only place you
Wish to go now.

Love opens new
Questions about old
Problems and gets
Easy answers for
The time being.

the ink bleeds

The ink bleeds through.
Smoke fills my lungs
And all I can do is
Think of her and
What might become
Of all of the madness.
Somehow I've made
It this far and
Now giving up is
All that's left to do.
So many times before
The pen I hold has
Shown me the way,
And with her it is
Suddenly blind and
Emphatically useless.

Past feelings erupt
Sending the only
Thing I hold dear
Into the dissection
Of thought that my
Mind has developed
To destroy any
Happiness that might
Ponder slipping in,
To maybe brighten
A dismal life of
Hell-bound shit.
There it sits on its
Mental pedestal I've
Created for it,
The only thing I hold dear.

waxy vision

A happy day comes
To a close

No more pot and
She's not home

Everything ceases to
Amaze me

Lovely ghosts play
With waxy vision,
Yet her face is
Always so clear

And she's there,
Right there for me

Unaware of all
The plans

naked vixen

Nothing to offer
And I offer it
All to you.
Hoping for some
Instant of insanity
On your part
To snatch up all
Of the nothingness
That stands in
Front of you.

A naked vixen
Of love captured
In a photograph
By the camera in
My mind so that
No other windows
May gaze upon it
But my own.

Owning a sick
Portrait of love
And guarding it
From everything
When nothing wants
It but my own
Lost sense of
Need that has
Blinded the
Important things
In my life.
You have replaced
It all.

insecurities disappear

Insecurities disappear into black nights
As the red fire approaches.
(E)steam rises through thoughtful misconceptions
Lost in hazy days of smoke
With nowhere to run.
Losing the light leaves darkness covered in contemplation.
The future is behind the lost souls
Looking forward for the lost light,
Losing the life.
Wills fly with courage and are copilots on
Mindless journeys to nowhere.
Glancing over smooth shoulders to see past it.
Finding the treasures of love lost.
Finding the treasures of lust lost.
Finding the treasures of life lost.
Wound in tattered cloth the mummy walks,
Living in death experiencing it all slow.
Flapping in the winds of despair and disappearing.
Lost are the happy days,
Always closing the sun.
Blackness of night enters and asks of some company.
It seems the sleepless dog even needs it.
Alone and wandering together through it all.
The night
       The mummy
              The treasures
Lonely and dying on mindless journeys to nowhere.

ninety-nine ways

Ninety-nine ways to blind the soul,
So many gone untouched.
Nothing can close what's been
Opened in a sad lonely man.
Sitting open to the world and waiting
For everything in him to disappear.
Leave crushed leaves behind as a
Sign of night's slumber,
Not wanting to be home.
Needing it to make wandering thoughts cease.
Allowing dreams to enter,
Take over these images and turn them
Twisting into mock films of perception.

The little boy's eyes meet the sad man's.
Pain and sympathy convey their messages,
Thoughts of what makes the sadness enter.
He'll remember the man.

Alone and sifting through the madness of loss,
Preparing for more of the same.
Storms of hatred and betrayal over nothing.
So many things could fill the voids.
Pockets of her trapped in his mind
Coming across them every now and again,
Opening worlds of regret with every snap.
Lost words find themselves in dreams,
Rise to be spoken
Forgotten with opening lids.
Sunshine kills the dreams.
Another lonely day awaits.

naked and on trial

Something happened to the mind
Losing everything
Naked and on trial for uncommitted crimes
Of commitment to a lost soul
That has everything ahead of it

Powerful music plays on
Drowns out the words
Echoing through the black hole
Of spite in the fragile mind of
The psychotic loneliness that
Breeds in cold dark places

Bring the beads and trinkets
Those lost along the road and collected
Put together in odd abstractness to
Form the worded art of a madman
With corridors of confusion built
To last through the insanity

Without a cause for life
Death enters

Take everything away and bear
This soul to show the
Last thoughts all related
Forever keeping her tied to
A heart that has a secret
Torture the prisoner
Words must spill quickly
To capture her
More clues in this endless
Investigation of the limits

Push the right buttons to
Unleash the night in fiery
Displays of torment and pain

Hanging plants of death to remind them
Her eyes dance like the
Fire that winks at you
From the top of wax mountains
Pain rises with the black smoke
Leading it into air surrounding
Thick with suffering
Impending tears that wait
To fall and see no chance
Of being born on the lonely nights
In the shadow of contemplation
That plays in the cold shiny room

To always be lost
Finds oneself.

saved

Save the hour.
Dance in midnight rains
Running down your face,
Reminding you of the
Tears that never fall.

Save the day .
Get stoned and let
The feelings fall.
Remember the love
Broken and in shambles.

Save the life.
Share the pain in ink,
Giving so much to
This lost soul
Searching redemption.
Loving her in false
Movies of the mind.

devil's slumber

And slowly evil wins.
Overcomes the being
That rests there with
Your soul at hand,
Squeezing it now and
Again to "grab" your attention.
Rising eyes meet and
Share the mutual pain
That flows in tattered
Hearts sleeping in the
Next room.
Awake and bring your
Tortured rays of beauty
That forever echo his name.

disturbing portrayal

Slow, kind death enters
Your thoughts as you
Begin to remember…

It meant nothing,
This disturbing portrayal
Of human emotion and
The thoughts of a psychotic
Played out on the
Screen in front of us.
Both of us wanted
To see it
It was nothing….

Slowly she pulled away.
Gazing into your eyes
She whispered those
Words of love.
Gently caressing her
In love.
Wishing for moments
Like these to go on
Forever
And now they do….

Always tormenting you
At the greatest times.
Disturbing your movement
Forward and away from her.
Lost in her forever and
Loving it.

a night at the circus

Bears will dance for you,
Clowns will juggle,
And there you will be with
Lights shimmering slightly in
Your eyes.
Allow them to have the
Appearance of love nearby
To spark the dreams and
Slow torture that
Destroys him as the heart
He holds dries out in
The desperate hour of
Darkness as the music stops.
Gives way to the shouts,
Applause, and cries of the
Children too young to understand
The meaning of the
Elephants that roamed
Around people and why
The family cat was
So small in comparison to
The ones there at the
Big top of madness.
So as we walk away from
The madness remember,
It was all for you.

whispered rumors

A condom wrapper lies at
The foot of the bed you
Died in and I'm lost.
Staring blankly at me
It whispers the rumors
That will haunt me forever.
Losing you is all that
Forever has left to
Offer and I'm tired
Of glancing at the
Merchandise that's priced
Too high to begin with.

Being in your life is
Heaven laid before me.
I haven't the
Courage to ask for
Acceptance into the
Kingdom of light that
Your memory has built
And now resides over
Nothing but a simple
Pawn in this game
Of life that you play.
Trying only for one thing,
To be loved by the
One that matters:
The queen.
And there upon the hill
She sits observing
The fire crested raven
That filtered my heart
Through a primeval sieve

That left nothing to
Her highness's liking.
Tossing the tattered
Leftovers aside for
The scavenging dogs.

The price was right the
First go 'round and
Now I'm broke
Trying to find a way
To purchase that bounty
In the window that
Calls to me through
The silence.

empty hook

So many fish in the sea but
No bait in the pail.
An empty hook floats to
The bottom where it rests.
Eyes glance in their sideways
Fashion and noses begin to rise
Only looking for a good fuck or
Money and neither are to be found.
Lost are the days of splendor
When nothing was right but
Everything was okay.
Death was on your side then.
Always waiting to be called upon
And always failing in its duties.
Luck has nothing to do with fishing
Yet every nibble signifies
A lucky day ahead.
Tossing the ones that lack
What she offered back.
Hoping someday to hook that
Same one sometime with
The empty hook that
Lies at the bottom resting.
Looking ahead in a dream state
That leads false hopes into play.
Images of the resting hook full
And dancing in hypnotic rhythms
To pull her away from the sea
And back into this heart.

laughing solemnly

Laughing solemnly and without care.
This subject binds you
By pushing you away
Into this void of confusion
Where everything makes sense
For a few wilting days.
Nothing means everything now,
It's all you own.
Keeping demons in and loving them,
Nurturing their hearts with the
Hatred that dances in your mind.
A loss of words leaves you at
The edge of eternity with
Two paths to choose from.
And in your hands lies
Your fate as menial as
Fridays and the boredom they
Bring with nothing but
Yourself and the problems
You hold to brood over.
Thinking only of the lost
Days where your heart still hides.
The only happiness in life
Is found through the heart
And yours lies hidden,
Calling to you from its
Dark lair of loneliness
Where forgetting only comes
In dreams and all you
Dream about is her.

shoulder of evil

Looking over the shoulder of evil
      wondering what it writes.

Feeling falls on paper and
      nowhere else.

The worst evil breeds hate
      while hiding in hearts.

Locked there by gods of love
      that watch it squirm and
            fight to live in boredom.

fire rises

Fire rises from the nose of the devil.
Hatred lies deep seeded inside.
Setting up situations of calm light
Only to destroy their subtle beauty.
So precise in argument,
So vain in delivery.
Responses of little smiles and false
Beliefs grate at it most
And still you live.
Live through it all hoping that
Somewhere lost in the future is happiness.
Wondering if looking back will ever
Be enjoyable, if it will shine back
The darkness of ill-fated arguments.
Those of expenditure and lost time,
Time spent sitting in boredom and silence.

Silence breeds many things.
Love and friendship are not
Among them.

Festering sores of life that
Multiply on the backs of some
Dwindling in size and number.
On others only leaving those
Stricken with poisoned
Blood of time and silence.

Still you sit,
Flashing little smiles,
Encouraging the inevitable.

gorge yourself

Slowly hell sets in.
The warmth encloses you,
Comforts your pain and worries.
Shows you death and asks
Of you to partake.
Stuffing yourself on the
Thought to the point of
Fullness that allows
Slumber to enter.
Softly your head hits,
Eyes close, and images
Bleed into darkness
Leaving you beckoning
The actions of the
Death that you have
Gorged yourself with.
Happy days are few.
Obsolete are the things
That held meaning.
Staring into the eyes
Of dark thought
Brings life to a point
Of do or die.
Easier the pain becomes.
Lost in it you sit,
Brood over the last
Bit of integrity that
Is quickly dwindling.
Points of loss,
Confusion, and future
Close in.
Show you in detail
The frailty of your meaning.

The words fall fine
On the white page
Spelling out the demise
Of this nation so strong
In its past.
Fleeting empire of pain,
Opening the door and
Resting the excuse of
Apology on the surface
Of a lifetime that is
As flat and boring as
The last months of
Filth you've wallowed in.
Trying for nothing is easy,
Caring for it bleeds you
So dry you lay on the
Bed you've created and
Die slowly.
Letting all that know
That this is theirs.

for sam

Climbing into the car,
Hatred of a mother
Driving a force up the hill
To be somewhat comforted
By a friend that pays
Back gas with the
Camel straights that
Would someday be
Your life's blood.
Endless conversations about
Nothing that fixed
Everything around you,
And on the cemetery
Hill in darkness a
Teacher was born.

Dark highway night.
Chicken grease still
Lingers in the air
As you pull off,
Making a journey
That had become
Ritualistic to the
Point of spiritual lifting.
As the destination
Neared and was then
Laid out in front
Of you the teacher appeared.
Smiles filled the back
Lot along with shouts
Of salutations erupting
From the face of the
Soon to be or currently

Impaired master greeting
His apprentice of life
The party will begin soon.

There guarding a doorway
That meant nothing in
A hallway that meant
Nothing yet held the
Mentor's life they
Would meet.
Stumbling up to one
Another and sharing
The firm handshakes
That were always
Followed by the phrase
"Smashing Pumpkins man!",
And the story of their
Chance acquaintance.
Who knows if anyone
Heard it.
It wasn't meant for that,
It was just theirs.

The student's eyes see
Many things,
Some of which aren't
Even real.
The teacher is needed
To help examine
Them with an older
Wiser view.
Teachers are hated,
Mentors loved.
Combining the two
In syncopated harmony

Leaves one wondering
If life is so complicated
After all.
Learning is needed and acquired.
Friendship is wanted and achieved.

Life was right for a time.
Only when your
Company was shared with
This person that opened
Your eyes to so much,
Introduced you to so much.
He is the door to
New worlds and you
Have the key.

shimmering life

Shimmering life of debt
Ending in one explosion
Of the mind.
Blitzing memory drowns
Out everything,
Leaves tonight and
Nothing else running
Through this jumble
Of thought.
Festering blights on the
Skin of eternity.
Loss controlling a life
Of confinement and
Your heart is denying
What it needs.
Old excuses run wild
With nothing to stop them.
Her face plasters
The walls of your
Dreamscape and there's
No escaping it,
This thing that's so
Needed in my life.

the sad mask

This sad mask that
Rides my face only
Hiding anger and pain.
I am the clown and
This is my show,
The usual thing
Juggling, jokes…..hatred.
Death defying feats
Of a lost puppy
Whining for its siblings.
Mother was lost long ago.
The dancing lies
The shaved poodles
The hidden love
They were all present
Sharing this experience
Of confusion.
Approaching games appear,
Taunting me with decisions.
Life is lost and
The red lips curve down.
This is my mask and
I am the clown.
She is my show.

pendulum

The pendulum sways
Back and forth
Allowing her memory
To rush in and
Torture me.
The way she felt
In my arms,
The kisses we
Shared for hours
On end,
Quiet times together
Gazing into each other's eyes.
Loosing myself in
Her was heaven.
The way our
Bodies fit tightly
Together as if meant
For just that.
The extra beats my
Heart had when she
Was near.
That was love.
This is love.
Every thought encompassed
In her image.
Death is sweet without her,
Beckons me through
The cracks of walls
That took so long
To erect.
Destroyed over eons
Of loss.
The false hopes

Shared throughout my being.
Dreams that keep it
All alive somewhere inside
Of this lost child.
The night comforts,
Calms the rocky expression
Of feeling that I'm
Lost in.
Forever trapped in my own hell.

rays of hope

Wax your bikini line,
Light will hit it
Where we're headed.
Soon worth will
Embrace our children,
Rays of hope will
Raise our babies.
New found life in
This new found land
And the scenery
Never changes.
Day after day the
Old runs on.
Spontaneity in shambles
Next to you begging
For the carpenter
In you to rise up
And assemble its
Broken meaning.
Sudden outbursts of
Life erupt scaring
The shit out of you.
Making you realize
That that's just
The way it works.
Enough to keep you
Going but not enough
To get it.

floating death

Floating death approaches
And floats on by.
Weaseling its way
Out of reach for
The last time.
This will be the
Last chance you
Give it to take
You away and your
Heart breaks with
The thought of
Not having it there.
You realize this
Isn't the last.
You've said that
Every time,
And still you
Wish to leave.

rubble

Greatest loss yet to
Befall the rubble
Of a man that you are.
Friendships die but
Not like this,
Not in a storm of
Blind accusation and pain.
Leaving him behind
Was never part of
Some master plan you
Hatched and yet
Neither was becoming
His life.
Too much stress.
Too much guilt.
Nothing is worth that,
Not even a wonderful
Friendship.
Going mad with
Frustration is not
Friendship.
Worrying what the
Other is thinking and
Never knowing is not
Friendship.
So what did we have?

smoke filled vacation

Wandering through oblivion
Thinking about nothing important.
Stumbling across memories
That choke the life
Out of death.
This, the only thing
That's left is no better.
Living hell after hell
That ended up a life.
Over and over in this
Mindless dreamscape
Trying to figure out
Why.
Lighting a cigarette for
Some time away from it,
Not allowing it to
Singe what's left.
Little mental escapes
That play as vacations
From the thoughts
That plague this place.
Alone and desperate
For a change
Which is never easy.
Gradually is shifty.
Suddenly is deafening in tone.
They all die lonely
And that's where it ends.

genesis

Yes this is where it begins.
Darkness falls and the
Eyes of the night start
To watch over you.
Slowly the death sets
In and all is forgotten.
What lies ahead is
What matters now and
That is nothing.

Yes this is where it was born.
Lasting beyond the
Rotting discharge of
Years past and the
Infuriating loss of
Night awakening you every
Morning with the
Bird's song amplied.
Cool air finding its way
Through it all and
To your skin now
Rough with tiny
Bumps of reply.

This is where it begins,
Yes this is the place.

voids of eternity

So here it is,
Alone in this
With no one to
Turn to for help.
The animals
Look upon you
As though they
Feel your pain
But for some
Reason don't care.
No help can
Come from them
And this they
Realize.
As for yourself
You look upon
Them as though
They feel your
Pain and you
Need that.
Someone to
Share it with,
Your friend.
Not only does
The loneliness
Burn it leaves
Voids of eternity
To remember
It by.

dream state

To be without leaves pain.
Feel this and live,
Keep it built
Then destroy it,
Life is the only trial.
This is your fight.
Bleeding will do nothing
And crying is useless.
Please take your life and leave me.
You dubbed this the end
Then revoked it as if I wouldn't care.
This is your dreamland now.
Life is your playground.
Take up your reigns and wander,
Live your dream within this dream.
Revel in its glory and be master
Over "their" actions.
Live that dream and come tell
Me of the outcome.
The results will be late
Or never materialize at all.
Man can handle only so much.

destruction

Life cast down to thee
And you destroyed it.
Friendships befall thee
And you spoil them without
Knowledge of your actions.
Did you expect it
To go easy?
Was it supposed to
Fall into place and
Work out swell?
Well of course it was!
Just like everything
Else in life....
What a fucking joke.
Life is a disease
You catch as a spirit.
There are treatments
But they cost so
Much you just suffer.
Trying to make it
To the next day
Knowing the disease
Has only worsened
And life is more
Like hell than the
Day before.
Just get used to it.

misty eyed

Misty eyed lake of fire
Burning always never brighter

Turning soon to gray-black ash
Swing around and grab your sash

Run from the darkening scene
Everything is so obscene

Slowly raise your bleeding hand

This is what remains here now
Long sad memories lost somehow

Please be gone into the night
Your bleeding hand he cannot fight

Lovely severed broken life
Quickly lost to you my wife

Leave the smile that tortures me
I'd like to look upon its glee

The bliss keeps pouring
We're still soaring

And slowly we will lose

predestined

After it all subsides
Will happiness enter?
It never really leaves
Just turns transparent.
Ghost like it sits
Watching all the chaos.
Shadows cover its presence
Hiding the long stares.
You're all it has,
The last thing left.
Life holds many empty
Glasses to show it,
And only one stands full.
Full of scarlet haired,
Love, and the meaning
Of life.
That line was of my wife.
You've been my wife
All along and we didn't
Even know it.
Life may be predestined.
Then where would we be?
Stuck waiting on it
To happen,
Never helping it along
At all.
Just waiting.

living memories

It all flooded back
Tonight, restored everything
We still have: nothing.
And yet everything is there
Playful little tickles, pokes
The way our bodies try to
Fit together without
Even touching.
And there you sat
So at home in the
Madness and looking
Like heaven on a
Brisk spring morning.
So corny the words
That flow from this mind
And you're the only
Thing on it.
Kiss me now when you
Should have
Back there on the
Bed where we were
Hidden,
Seen only smoking
Our cigarettes and
Sharing conversation.
Rest your head on
My chest so I can
Caress your hair.
I used to love that,
The way your hair
Felt in my fingers.

small boy

I saw myself as a small
Boy that day staring
At you in the store.
Such innocence lacking
Knowledge of what
Beauty was so I just
Stared at you.
How could someone
So beautiful be sucked
Into this.
The entire moment
Left this boy confused,
Sad, and somewhat empty.
Stepping into him is
What you've done.
Hearts dangle on thin
Wires and await a breeze.
Love me now or never
And hold this little boy,
Convince him of your
Love and I will follow.
You see he senses what
Life has blinded.
Makes real what has
Become dreams and
Tells me I need you.
But wanting you has
Hurt me too much.
As fire dances around
In scarlet tendrils
Of beauty
I am yours forever.

highway solitude

Headed down self-destruction's
Highway and it feels
So right.
Tonight is the night,
Slowly is the only way
To go.
Speeding down the
Freeway of life and
It's killing me so
Quickly.
Lost is what I feel
Around you.
The moon is in your
Heart and it's been
So long since daylight.
Keep running until
The boarder is reached,
Tell her I said hi
And let nothing go
Unsaid.
She needs to see it.
My soul is on display
Now….for everyone
To see and I'm dying.
She is everything to me,
Holds my life in
Solitude along with
The soul you stole
So long ago.
The rabbit is rabid
And the wolf is tame.
My life is boredom and
So much goes on in it.

closed eyes

Why is it that
Every time I close
My eyes you're there?
Maybe the time
Spent was too good,
And then maybe
You're mine forever
And just don't know it.

convincing yourself

Do you think you'll ever
Get over her?
No….not in this life.
There's really no need,
As time goes on i
Find more ways around her
But i've yet to find
The way over.
Just a pawn in this game.
She'll do as she pleases
And that's all right with me.
If i never reenter her
Life then at least
She'll have made it
Her own decision.
Loneliness has become
A way of life.
Nothing can comfort
The dying child
In its time of need,
And nothing is all i
Have without her.

lost freaks

Seeing double ,
Unable to move.
There's two of
You and I'm in bliss.
Slowly I rise,
Thinking of all
The times I've
Been like this.
Lost in the bottle
With nothing to do
But brood over all
The lost time.
We should still
Be together,
Roaming in life
With nothing
But each other to
Believe in.
Religion creates chaos
And starts wars.
Makes those who
Follow mad with
Thought and plan.
Conversions of those
That differ rattle
In their brains.
The freaks that
Resist are condemned
And judged,
Ridiculed for their
Life.
We're all lost freaks.

young warrior

Staring death in the eyes made me chuckle.
Riding at the pale horseman's side sends
Exhilarating tingles of joy throughout the
Body of the empty passenger,
Letting him out just short of his destination.
The journey to the secret city of fire
Is rocky and seldom traveled.
His shoes are tattered and worn when the
Doorway of the queen is reached.
Dry cracked knuckles rap on the wood.
"This is where I was sent.
Was told paradise is kept here
Protected by fires that fall around the
Pale face of love."
"I can see heaven in the eyes of my angel.
So what's on the other side?"
There's a password of faith to be had.
His mouth opens but nothing pours out,
Silence is friend turned enemy in a
Desolate wasteland of fear.
Nothing leads to desire for everything.
Keep this secret hidden well within the
Confines of your heart young warrior.
This is what love is all about,
Feeling the beat of loss in an empty heart
And he's liking the music it spills out in return.
Put your head here.
Listen to the vibrations,
The soft lullaby of pain.

soft journey

Soft journey through sleepless night
Death's figure at your side.
Pray for daylight to end the pain.
Your angel's voice echoes.
Nothing is the same anymore.
Only wisdom you can see
Comes from the mind of a madman
Dancing naked in wilting fields of lust.

You wish for death then laugh.
You want to die and join your demons.
Fire breathing generals guard your
Sacred door of hate.
The confusion sets in much too late.
With heavy heart you lay to rest
The current chapter and ponder the next.
Its words,
Its fashioning,
Your angel's glances shimmering.
Nothing seems to die like love,
So slow and unyielding
Torturing the souls of ravished hands.

Sleep is so clever and indecisive
When the master is at bay.

hypnotized

Midnight movies lighting up
The mind's horizon.
Everything is good there.
Happiness is what it should be.
Pain is captured in void
No need for the release.
This is the keepers land
All is upheld.
Lawless existence of conformity
Roaming slowly through a
Black stone garden of expression.
Thoughts at the time
Shape the scripts of this film,
The ending happy.
Always beginning with exhaustion.
Creeping eyes of the panther;
Hypnotized.

desolate

I looked out today
Over what has become
My life and began to
Laugh somewhat uncontrollably.
It seems that
Everything ahead of
Me are the dreams
Of yesterday and
The nightmares of my
Past are still
Haunting the desolate
Present.
Hold this tortured
Soul in your arms and
Consume its sobs.
Feel this pain that
Surrounds me in the air,
Breathe it.
Taste the dish
Prepared by my hands
From a recipe of fate
Passed down from
Generation to generation.
A secret well kept
Hidden by the knowledge
That it all passes and
Makes you a stronger
Person.
Heartache, loss, the
Unattainable desires
That taunt the
Chefs of hell's
Kitchen just linger there.

The highways of life
Call to me.
To be away is what
Leads me to insanity.
The reaching out into
Nothing, swearing my
Fingers brushed something
Toys with me.
Happiness now hidden in
A heart that has no
Key but decays over
Time becoming closer and closer
To falling open at my feet
Beckons me.
To be ready for it
Is impossible and yet
Here I am rushing to
Get the items I need
For its arrival,
Hoping it waits if the
Deadline is broken.
And this is all my
Life has become.

stained hands of hate

Elegance knows no boundaries,
Gets lost in her.
Eternities spent on this perfection.
Maturity wanders lost backroads
Dumping its loot on anyone near it.
As its back weakened
She was at its side.
Following lost guidance of the
Heart to find ones' self leaves
You with stained hands of hate,
Wishing for the new arrival of
Warm rain to wash away
The thoughts.

struggle continues

Stepping into the night
Searching for anything
To grasp onto for strength

Keeping sane has become
The struggle of life

Getting away from her
Has become a task

Neither needs to be completed
Nor left untouched

Needing her is what
Keeps sanity here

Without a cause
Nothing is worth death

With her death is a
Sweet faced child
That calls to this
Man from far off
Deserts of loss

Wandering through
This night the
Struggle continues

face of divine will

Self-destruction seems
Inevitable,
Smells so sweet.
Death comes to those
Who least expect it.
It's my playmate.

Dancing on fire we
Dart in and out of
Its grasp teasing it.
My eyes bleed as you
Put your hand in
His, yet he's transparent.

Feel the face of divine will.
Grasp at its coattails and follow.
It takes you nowhere.
Exactly where you need to be.
The eyes of fright burn you
Leaving scars on the only thing left.
This is what eternity has given you.
A vast majority of pain with
Happy intermissions of sanity,
Enough to keep you living.

The bottle....
A friend of the past revisited.
It drowns out your sorrow
Making you see the answers
More clearly.
Bitter sweet burning of
The throat as you realize
It's taking effect.

She's calling to you.
Soft sweet voice
Of drunkenness.
Everything wonderful is
Now doubled and the
Answers are all clear
As you dance with
Your friend and the bottle.

You <u>can</u> see heaven
In the eyes of
Your angel,
And there's nothing
On the other side.

other times there is too little

So many questions torture my mind and
Now you need the answers to them?
Tell me this,
Something new or maybe just forgotten.
Love is a strange thing.
Sometimes appears nonexistent,
Other times there is too little
To cover everything that desires it.
How I wish I could answer the
Questions that haunt my dreams
And wander your mind.
If feelings could be murdered
There would be massacres of
Emotion throughout my being,
If only….
Yet I stand before you in
Torn agony over where you "stand"
And where she will always reign.
Nothing could lesson what I
Feel for you and yet I'm
Frightened by the thought of
Never loving another again.

This is my hell.
Welcome to my shattered heart.

lost in slumber

Her cigarette lies stifled
In a candle that has been
Used by company as an ashtray
For what seems like years.
I confuse her.
She can't read me like the others
She's been around.
That's good I suppose.
I've spent most of my life
Becoming a book that's in a
Language only my mother
Can understand,
And even she stumbles now and again.
All the time spent talking to
This women tonight left me
Relieved and somewhat exhausted.
Too many questions that couldn't be answered.
So many doubts about what we were doing.
She has a child at home asleep and
Has to get back to it.
The smile on her face as we kissed
Made me remember one similar.
We rose and I walked her to the
Door across a fluffy carpet and we
Shared one last kiss as
She rushed home to her beautiful
Child lost in slumber.

how you played

I'm sure you played beautifully tonight.
Walking out, I can imagine, in that black
Dress that stops just below the knees.
Correcting your bow to position,
Waiting on the order of a man that
Has no purpose and total control.
I can imagine the spectators' reactions
As you emerged from the back with
Hair the color of sunset and eyes
Sparkling like diamonds.
The way you play captivating them
Somehow drowning out everything else
As though it's your solo.
Or maybe that's just the way it
Appears to me when I watch you play.
Remembering the way you smiled my direction
When you noticed I had actually shown up.
Why wouldn't i?
What more reason do I need?
I imagine when the music stopped
They all applaud you and none other,
Or maybe that's just the way I applaud
When I watch you play.
I'm sorry I didn't make this one.

sheeted world

She wants something
That I can't give
Her for no reason at all.
Feelings should've
Passed by now,
They should've
Disappeared in
The past that
Has now become
My hell.
Laying with beautiful
Women should
Heighten ones
Spirit.
I think this
As mine crumbles
In her arms.
My spirit was
Taken with neither
Consent or offering long ago.

12 pack under the bed,
Don't let him see,
I'm just a gopher
In this sheeted world.

Tears begin to fall
As I hold her and
It's been so long
Since that happened
That I'm startled.
No more emotion
In the form of

Simulated eye rain
Was going to fall as
A cause of what my
Demon had done.
I promised myself that
Yet here I stand
Crushing the heart
Of another beautiful
Woman and it shatters
Me on the inside.
Tanks roll in on the
Coasts of orient
Shores and all I can
Do is be haunted
By a past I've tried
To escape for centuries.
Always adding to this
Fragile soul another
Stab.
Wishing to die in
The arms that held
Me last night.

blurry haze

People crowded into one
Live party all wasted,
Young and dancing.
Think of this as you
Look to old friends,
Now lovers for short
Periods of time.
Lost souls just
Searching for a song
And all of it in
A blurry haze of
Pharmaceuticals now
Rushing through your
Veins replacing what
Was once blood.
You glance to the
Side at a point to
See an old flame.
It's been stifled
So you move on,
Moving to your
Car where you
Degrade yourself and
The woman at home.
Thinking about you
With that old friend
And new temporary
Lover as she whispers
Let's get in the back seat.

strangers

There they were,
Just sitting enjoying
Their meal and she
Was beautiful.
They like your hair
So you sit with them
And your coffee to
Chat for a little while.
So easy to share
With them.
You've known them
Forever it seems,
And lose yourself
In their conversation
And her beauty.
She has a gem
Attached to her
Belly and shows
It to you.
Funny really how you
Reached for it like
There was no such
Thing as personal space,
Wishing at the same time
That you could be the
One to caress that
Torso tonight finding
New love in a gem
And smile.
You rise instead and
Comment on the irony and
Leave the strangers there.

lost in it

Lost in friendship and a cup of coffee.
Angels surround me yet heaven is
Nowhere in sight.
Foreigners all around and it's mind freeing.
Come with me to this new land,
Laugh out loud,
Shout with glee.
This is where we will stay.
Conversations and missing souls,
They stare at the freakish style
Wishing for the young freedom
That was lost in the years.
Pain and heartache snatches their lives.
Here is where they swap stories.
Keeping their sanity is easy,
They've endured the worst.
All that's left is death
And here we sit lost in friendship
Loving life.

blind or crazy

The stranger is on my mind again.
The gorgeous stranger,
The one that looked to me and
Told me I was beautiful.
I think now as to if she
Was blind or just crazy.
Others have backed her story.
I wonder if the whole
World has gone mad as i
Look to the mirror and
Realize that it must have.
Her gemmed abdomen still
Etched in my mind.
How can something like that,
A creature made only by
God's own hands be so blind?
Am I the one that's crazy?
Have I slipped into a parallel
Dimension where front is back,
The hideous is the divine, and
The drug addicts are the rulers
Of worlds yet to be found and
Conquered?
These questions riddle me
As the stranger wanders my mind.

despised feelings

I lay on my bed
Despising my feelings.
She tells me she
Wants to love me
And I can't stand it.
How to tell someone
That you don't want
To be with them
Because your
Emotions won't allow
You to do so.
It sounds so cheap,
The easy way out.
I never thought it
Would be this serious
And now I'm buried.
She wanted to be blunt
And I allowed her to be,
Only now this doesn't
Seem like dating.
Promises also haunt me.
Never again,
Not with a friend,
And now here I am
Breaking that promise.
Leaving this shallow
Boy with the hardest
Decision in the world.
Let it go on and
Try to change these
Feelings or cut it off
Now and spare both
Of us the pain.

I've never ached
Like this before.
So many mixed emotions,
Searching for so long.
Commitment the goal.
Now I have it and
It hurts too much
To keep alive.

God if you're listening
Spare this soul and
Breathe life into this
Friendship.

I'm a sorry fool.

prince in keeping

Asking for nothing
As I walked into it all.
The words flowed
Out of our mouths
Like the birds from
Spring trees in
Full beautiful bloom.
Chatting with Satan
And his lovely demons.
The blond caressed
My greasy locks and
Captured me in her
Elegance as the
Raven haired one
Helped the dark
Prince in keeping
My mind alive.
If hell is where
She is kept with
Pink gems as the
Tie between these
Worlds then I
Follow.
Blind like the
Raving madman
Screaming for his
Mother or God or
The woman who
Keeps him tied
To life,
Temporarily forgotten.

2:50

Somewhere on a dark
Country road just outside
Of town.
Somewhere near a place
Called steel bridge.
She used to party there.
We climb into the back
Of her truck as my
Hands move all over
Her body.

"I don't care what you
Say I want you to
Make love to me!"
But I'm too drunk
So my hands move
All over her body.

Soon it's time to
Go home,
2:50.
We pull our
Clothes back on
And climb into
The cab as she
Drives me back
To my car.

Drunkenly I drive
To my cup of
Coffee just to think.

porcelain god

Absent minded
And dying.
Coughing up lungs
And pissing from
Cock-flesh half
Dead with the
Taste of whiskey.
I sit back and
Doubt God again
Which only makes
Me feel stupid and guilty.
Coughing up more
Lung I slip
Into unconsciousness
With strangers on
My mind.

days pass

The days pass
And I think of her,
That stranger which
Showed me what
Beauty truly was.
The gem, the gem
Is what is bore
Into my mind and
It only equals
One tenth of her
Beauty.
Only three days
And I'll see her
Again.
Be able to slip
Into her eyes.
Those eyes drew
Me to her.
The little smile
She flashed just
Made me wonder
What life would
Be with her and
God help me
I'm going to find out.
Only three days.

otherworldly

She called me again
From wherever her kind
Come from, Harrison I think.
It has become a welcomed
Nuisance, something new.
"Are you still beautiful?"
She asks.
If I ever was then yeah,
Those words still baffle me.

In the coffee house
This little girl with
Pigtails too high on
Her head stares at me,
Then I stare at her, and
We stare at each other.
She smiles,
Then I smile, and
We both stare at
Each other and smile
While I smoke my cigarette.
The whole thing reminds
Me of the stranger.

"Can I call you back
Another day?"
"From Harrison?"
"Yeah?"
"Sure?"
"When will I ever see
You again?"
Who knows,
But I'll see the stranger in 2 days.

secrets

She makes me giggle
Like small children
Chasing fireflies in a
Field on cool summer nights.
This is their neon Vegas and
She is mine.
Put it all on black 9.
Winner to the man
With the great big smile!
What's your secret?
See the angel standing
By the slots?
Yeah.
Now it's no secret.
The winning streak
Continues and the
Children have finally
Cracked the insect's
Flashing code.
Now they have
Mason jars full of them
To carelessly leave on
The window sill to
Back in the 3:00 sun,
Only to empty them
At 9:00 to start again
In the black night.
Put it all on black 9.

moving to the beat

Her eyes pierce mine and I
Think I see love dancing in them.
Forever seems like such a short
Period of time when I think of her.
There should be more.
Love hasn't danced for me in so long,
Mostly just lays there lifeless.
Now along comes a beat it can really
Move to and I'm afraid that I might
Scare it off by being so blunt.
But if she gets away I'll never
Forgive myself.
So maybe I should slow down.

chance meeting

It was odd really
Sitting there with
One eye on the
Death and resurrection,
The other searching for
Beauty that's nowhere
In sight.
Somewhere behind me I think.
She seemed so excited and amazed
To see me.
All three of them did.
I gave my word and I kept it.
Besides how could such a lovely
Creature and interesting minds
Be let go on only a chance meeting
And a cup of coffee?
Remembered only by a braid
Which had to come out 3 days after.
These are the greatest strangers.
It would take novels to tell
Of all they offer and
Frankly I don't have the patience.

She makes me so happy and
It's been a long time.
Maybe she's my savior.
My deliverance into a state of
Permanent and perpetual bliss.
To be lost there forever.
Long after I get boring and
Am forgotten.
Long after the shattered heart
Heals and I'm left in this

Place wearing nothing but the
Smile she has so delicately
Painted on my mask.
When I remove it will it
Have soaked through and
Stained my soul.
Hope strains to answer
Such odd questions, and
All it can give are estimates
And misplaced guesses.
Right now it whispers yes.

the jockey

He was a racer of horse
Rolling down the highway
With his horse trailer.
Probably holding 2 of the
Finest fillies in the state
And he wasn't from this one.
On the back of his truck
Was sitting his carriage,
Red seat with black trim.
I wondered if he raced them
Himself or maybe had his
Son in on it.
So many little questions
About a man I knew nothing of
And would never see again.
Just for now on this highway.

shake me

Heartache, heartbreak

Child come and wake me
       shake me
              break me
                     take me
To your grassy meadows
Full in bloom under a
Summer sun with the
Scents of angels and buttercups

Young lovers roam and frolic
In the misty air

Heaven lies here and we've
Found it

dirty window

The cigarette that burns
Reminds me of all the lives that
Are slowing falling apart
As I stare out this dirty window
From a room full of music
That bores me, having been
Listened to countless times.
All that's left in their melodies
Are reminders of the past and
I've been trying to forget it for years.
The words are all memorized
And if I could play an instrument
Then the notes too would be lost
In my mind
Finding their way out at odd
Hours of the night and early morn
Causing the neighbors to pound
On these thin walls that have
Become my voluntary prison.
The bottle stares at me half full
Or half empty however you wish
To see it and I'm too drunk
To hold on tight enough to
Pour it into my now dry mouth.
And as I stumble to stare through
The dirty window I realize my
Life is okay in this thin prison
Trapped alone with the music
That bores me and the lives going
To hell outside so I pass out
With my ass half exposed to
The bumpy white plaster ceiling
On a bed that's too comfortable.

lament the lovers

My heart goes out to the lovers
That have to sneak around and
Lie to the masses because of an unwanted
Wife sitting states away.
or
The work place full of noisy people
That don't have anything in their lives
Worth talking about so they talk
About these wonderful lovers.
or
The mother that worries too
Much about her lovely daughter
Enough to drive her away over it.
My heart goes out to the lovers
Yet I envy their joy and happiness
Which is all I can see when I turn
To look at them.
So what I have to say is this
Forget the wife, to hell with the
Coworkers, love your mother no matter
What she does or how much she
Worries and enjoy your happiness.
The past is the past,
Nothing can change it.
No one knows what the future holds
So wait.
Live the moment and enjoy it
Worrying causes wrinkles and I
Think you're both too beautiful
To ruin yourselves with cracks
Of despair.
My heart goes out to the lovers.

unfitting symbol

A band wraps around the smallest
Appendage of a hand that caresses
The body that put it there.
Small silver with a design that can't
Quite be made out interrupted by
Black thread making the fit tight.
So small and beautiful it
Represents everything shared between
The two, with a past hat has
Nothing to do with them.
So odd how much something can
Mean and not mean all at once.

jealousy

Jealousy ruins many wonderful things
As it feeds on the immaturity that
Gave it birth and keeps it thriving.
No one knows quite where it comes from
Or what causes it yet it affects every
Human on the face of the earth at
Some low meaningless point in their life.
You may be the bearer or the receiver or
Maybe someone just in the way,
Caught in an evil crossfire of stupidity but
The eyes of jealousy will watch you at
That point and laugh.
Giggle with glee as it looks upon its doings:
Lives crumbling, tears falling, hearts breaking,
Friendships dying, and loves dwindling.
All of these and more.

For nothing except the simple pleasure of
Giving immaturity an existence.
If you are strong the eyes grow
Weary and they bore with your solid mind,
Moving on to the next weak and meager
Soul to watch its destruction take hold.
Ruining it all as it cackles.

Do you realize how idiotic you appear or
Have the hands of this beast blinded you?
Do you realize how little it affects me and
Have you been lost in anything before?
Something that drags your mind away
Form the past for the first time in years?
And are you even listening.

car

It's four wheels and an engine.
If lurches down the road
Due to a computer illness
In its dash.
It cost me more than I have
Yet I scrimp to keep it.
Its weather stripping is
Tearing off the drivers
Side and it rattles from
The inside.
It has no stereo,
That died about three
Weeks back.
There's rust, not a lot,
On the tip of the bottom.
The paint job is ruined from
Bird shit that was left
On too long.
The interior is dirty,
Dusty, and muddy.
There's a portable radio
In the backseat to make up
For the in dash death.
It reminds me
Of white-trash heaven and
Trailer park hell.
There are cigarette burns
All over.
Some from friends
Some from drunk guys
That had no business
Even walking.
Some say it's junk

Others call it luxury.
All I know is that it
Gets me from point A
To point B and that
It's just a car.

miscommunications

From the dirty window
Floats the screams of
Angry lovers.
His voice is clear from
The parking lot where
He stands.
Hers muffled from the
Inside of the truck,
Still running, signaling
That only one of the
Two will be staying
Here tonight.
The words he speaks
Make me think that
I may be in the same
Position on down the road.
So many miscommunications
Led to this moment.
His words make this known
And I fear the silence that
Tore them apart.
The entirety of the
Scene finally ending with
The truck speeding off
(Only the woman inside)
Brings questions rushing
Into my mind.
Will I ever become boring
To her,
Making her search for another?
Will the silence ever
Sneak into our lives
Causing us to think things

That aren't true and
See things that don't exist?
Does love die and will ours?
Can I always keep her satisfied
And will she always be there?

me, myself and i

There was nothing to be done
So to fend off boredom i
Began talking to myself.
They say the greatest gift
Is communication and without
It things crumble.
So with this thought i began
To communicate with myself
Just to keep our relationship stable.
The one between myself and i.
As the conversation deepened i
Found myself to be rather boring
And wondered how anyone could
Stand to be around either myself or i.
At times i guess it was an
Okay discussion and i wondered
Who was doing the talking
Myself or i.
One of us had to die but
In fear of killing the interesting
One i decided against it and
Lit another cigarette hoping
Someday for myself's sake that
i would develop a personality.
Or vice versa whichever the
Case may be.

lovely day out

So this is where it ends.
Sitting with nothing more
Than clouds, cigarettes, and words.
There is a face in the clouds,
I think it resembled one
Of your forefathers then
Slowly it contorted into the
Face of an ape man then to ape
Reverse evolution.
Is this what awaits us?
Have we evolved to a point
Where there is nothing left
But what's behind us?
Do we have to go back?
Can't we just stay here
Trapped in this gloomy day
With the cirrus and cumulous
Telling our future or our end?
To the right of it all, there
In the clearing where sun
Breaks through.
What is it?
A doorway maybe.
For who....our gods?
Don't guess just look to
The clouds for the answers.
Ask the questions while you
Still can.

eighteen years of sadness

Happiness found me in the eighteenth year
Making me wonder how someone could
Stay so unhappy for so long and I
Think I miss it.
Nothing can change how this life
Has been lived and even if it could
I don't think I would allow it.
How can I tell happiness of everything
That has shaped me,
Made me this bitter
Untrusting person that it loves?
Where would one start and does it
Even need to know?
It never had an existence in my
Life and now that's all that
Survives here.
Songbird songbird sing me your song
Nothing more beautiful and unending.
Lend me this time to gaze at you,
Get lost in your song and see
Visions of futures and offspring.
Why did it take you so long?

speeding through the rain

Water droplets pass me
In a horizontal fashion.
Highway winds force things
To change in unique ways.
Faces appear where beings
Could never rest their
Tired weary bones.
Worlds unfold like maps
Living the lives of many.
Watching as a god would
With its hands tied as
The world dissolves
In front of them.
Drunken eyes see things
Sober ones miss and yet
None of them seem
To be the important ones.

old faces new times

Old faces, new times
New loves, old feelings.
Same old two to nine.
New emptiness in the pockets,
New place to sleep,
Old mattress that knows me,
Old body, new age,
And everything's still the same.
Nothing really changes
In this world.
Nothing is ever really
New, just dressed up
A little.
Want leads nowhere
Except to the next
Level of want and
That to always wanting more.
Needing it all and never
Having anything,
Just a little more
Than what you had before.
I seem to have given
That up though.
I'm striving for the
Next level but only
Because life is making me,
Not because I want to.

If the want is lost
Then does death soon follow.

new nation

Mind-fucked generation
Lost in pills, the bottle, and herb.
Falling gracefully into a state
Of altered thought that
Let's them block out everything
In the world.
They may miss some good
But they're bypassing all
Of the bad.
Coping with lost degeneracy
And still not caring
What will become of the
New nation.
What will the world turn
Into years from now
When the mind-fucked generation
Takes the wheel.
And where will they be
When they sober up.

pickle

Brown filthy water
Surrounds it,
Keeps it safe in
Its gallon home.
Life has never
Been without it,
Wouldn't know what
To do without it.
Means nothing to everyone,
Means everything to me.
Of the two of us
I often sit and
Ponder if it's seen
More than myself.
The years it sat
In the corner of
A room that was my
Own and at the same time
Wasn't mine at all.
We've never spoken
To each other
(I'm just not the type I guess)
Still I know everything
About it.
So I'll keep it around
For a while longer.
Anyway I'd miss the
Talks the two of us
Never shared alone in
My room,
Just my pickle and me.

apostles and profits

The day sends down injustice
To calm the night following.
Come with me to meet
The master of ages,
Ask the questions that
Toll your weary mind.
Thoughts roll on and
Never ceasing fight
To end a relished life.
Leading once into temptation.
It's a peaceful place to
Dwell at times and
Keeps the tongue caught
In traps of reason and logic.
Listen to feel the
Power of lightening fire
Surging through the body
In a midnight hour
As rain begins to fall
On faces dry from
Penning words that spill
From it in slurred magnitude.
Tears form slightly hidden
By sweet drops of lost
Feeling from a god that
Keeps it all hidden,
Lost in pages and words.
Apostles and prophets,
Fire and brimstone,
Sweet liquid with pills.
Lost children in blind eyes,
Crying in hymn.

navigation

Lost in angelic presence
Waiting on the waitress
Dallying with orders backed
Up to touch the dawn.
Ours is buried somewhere
In it all and my stomach
Is the only sensor strong
Enough to detect its coordinates.
Nearing, nearing ever so slowly.
Mouth waters for it and
More so for her.
So elegant and sensual.
Taking her fills my thoughts,
But then where would we be?
What would we have?
To keep it at a distance gives
It a ghostly shawl to
Hide under and be mysterious.
To take and enjoy it, to
Throw off the shawl would
Leave it ruined.
The mystery that is.
Does love wilt in its grace?
Is it a chance we should take?
The flow is slowly pulling
The shawl away and
I'm just going with it.

god's tears

Too many secrets
Too many stars
Teardrops fall like rain
And god has nothing
To cry about

Pillar of darkness
Pillar of light
It came to me in
Midnight fright
The barrel tastes
So sweet
The knife just
A messenger of truth
The pills catching
Slightly while they
Go down
Keep me here
Tonight
Just for now.

further down the road

Doing forty in a thirty
And the only thing
In sight is a church
Sign preaching at me.
It speaks of what
I'm in and what I
Don't hold it says,
'There is no fear in love'.
Nothing more but
It's enough.
All this man needs
Now to figure out
What it is I fear.
Death was always
Frightful but just
Another toy unseen, unheard.
Disappointment
That I might be
One to somebody,
Now I don't really care.
Nothing to do but forget it.
'There is no fear in love'
So simple and complicated.
What now?
Further down the road
At fifty it occurs to me
There's a cop ahead
To the right.
I'm not worried though,
'There is no fear in love'.

lonely souls

Insomniacs and partiers,
Maybe a few lonely souls.
That's all that comes
To this coffee joint
At this time of night,
Or morning there's no telling
It might be 3:30 or 4:00
Maybe even 5:00.
Who knows, I stopped
Keeping track of it
All so long ago that
Nothing seems real
Anymore and the only
Thing that exists
Is reality.
You can at least
Tell the partiers from
All of the others.
The partiers stare
At us oddly,
Wondering how and why
Anyone would be in
This greasy joint
This late or early.
Some of us just
Can't sleep and
Some of us just
Don't have anyone.
Some of us fall into
Both categories.
I'm still trying to
Find out just which
One I fit in.

lost simple ways

Wasted memory.
The things that don't
Matter seem to be
Most important.
Remembering what they
Seemed to be then and
What they appear to
Be now.
It's always worse
In hind-sight, the
Only way to see things
Clearly here in the
Lost simple ways.
Keep quiet.
Hide the secrets of
Past, present, and
Soon to be inside.
The windows are
Open and your soul's
A book, but no one
Knows the language.

patriot

"I want you!"
He says with his
Splendid white beard,
Patriotic top hat, and
Bony finger of death
Stretched out toward
Every soul that
Happens by.
You may want me but
You'll never get me
You patriotic brainwashing
Bastard son of hypocrisy.
My grandfather always
Said, "Want in one hand,
Shit in the other.
See which one fills up quickest."
Family is sacred and
Here he is claiming
To be my uncle.
For some reason I don't
Believe my family would
Hand me a gun
Turn me to a jungle,
Or desert, or tundra
And say kill everyone
You see in clothes
Different from your own.
He wants my death.
My name on a wall
On a rock in a field full
Of them where they
Might come on the
Day of remembrance

And lay flowers on
My rock to pay homage.
He wants me to fight
For a country that he stole
So that no one else can
Steal it from him.
We all live on tainted
Soil and everyone will pay.
He wants me and
I hear Mexico is nice
This time of year.

greasing the wheel

It is love that starts wars
And nothing more
Be it the love of money,
Land, power, status
Or the love of another
It makes the world
What the world is
Maddening
Love drives men to death
The women it lifts to
Higher levels and makes
Them better people
Live with it a while
In the filth of poverty
With only the two of you
And nothing more
Feeding and surviving
Off of this notion
That no one can trace
To origin and no one
Can control
Then thinking no one
Has probably ever tried.

uncertain parenthood

She sits across from me
Sipping her coffee,
Smoking, and finishing her book.
It's good she says; fiction.
I don't care for fiction
That much so I don't
Suppose I'd like it,
But I could be wrong.

So many things occur
In mornings that are
Empty and somewhat boring.
She may be the mother
Of my first.
The biggest mistakes
Of my life will be
Shattered by this.
The greatest joys in
My life could be
Shadowed by this in
Its overwhelming happiness.

Things happen in the
Throws of passion.
Some you regret and
Others you wish to
Wallow in for days.
And what would mother
Say to the fact that
Her grandbaby was
Conceived in her bed.
Should she ever discover
The fact.

If anyone could be the
Mother of my children
Then I guess I've found her.
No one else has crossed
My mind before for that
So I guess she's the one,
The only one.
I just hope our children
Can fight her taste
In music.

"Yes I do love her why?"
"Just asking."
Well don't. Doesn't it show?"
"Yeah I guess so."

midnight hour

Midnight hour,
Fight the power
Lingering in the air.
Feel the thrill,
The one of after-kill
With bloodstained
Cement beneath.
Summer heat make
The scarlet drops rancid,
Smells so sweet.
Kiss the ground,
It's yours now.

blonde savior

Was everything I've ever felt a dream?
What was real and was it my reality?
Memories come flooding back and I don't
Really remember any of them clearly.
The minds of certain men are
Car crashes and Yahtzee games.
Things get thrown and jumbled
You're left to sort out the pieces.
Good in one pile slowly forgotten,
Bad in dreams you can't shake.
Lost in confusion of what is and is not,
Tormenting hell of life living hatred.
Shrinks and drugs help to sort it all out
Or maybe just help to hide it all.
New questions keep arising and no one's
Around to answer them.
Your soul aches with thoughts you
Can't control or forget.
Insomnia still cradles you in its arms.
Its voice resembles mother's so you're
Comfortable there in a peaceful land
Of nothingness.
She's your savior,
In front of you with blonde locks.
She'll save you and keep you sane.

nonchalant-ness

As she reads the words
It cuts deep,
Too deeply to imagine
Everything about my first.
The red hair,
The nonchalant-ness of the
Whole experience,
The pain it caused,
All of it rushing back.
But there's no time
To dwell or wallow
In it.
It's mine and all
Trapped inside.
The memories, the love
They're all in the
Past and all the past
Holds is history.
So many kinds of it and
This kind only
Matters to me.
I long for dark rooms.

corner seat

Nothing here in the coffee shop,
Just this sorry unemployed wretch
Of a man writing mindless words
In an almost full notebook
Wondering if he'll make rent or not.
His woman says she'll help but
Pride gets in the way of so many
Easy plans nowadays it's humorous.
Death still stalks him.
The only difference is he's not
Asking it to take him now.
Mother is still raising her skirt
For him to hide under and he's
Still trying to run from it.
Nothing here but the sad poet
With sad eyes.
People look at them and know
He's either wise or worn down.
So much has happened to him
And it shows.
All the jobs in the world
Couldn't change this situation
Or the fear he's a father.
So the coffee still keeps coming
And the problems still stir in
His mind as the sad poet with
Sad eyes hides in the corner
Of this coffee shop where
Nothing resides.

in the clouds

It was hot out that day.
The sky was full of big
Cumulonimbus clouds bringing
The rain that would only
Make everything sticky with humidity.
The tops were cut off of them
By the passing jet stream
And all I could think
About was how much
This job sucked and how good
The cigarette in my hand was.
It was the last smoke break
Of the day, the last smoke
Break I would ever have here
In this hell on a receiver.

It was hot out that day,
Eighty maybe ninety.
I was nauseous from it.
That and the other workers
Bitching about how much
They hated the supervisor
And the job but needed
The paycheck.
I figure that there's other
Paychecks and the supervisor
Can kiss my ass.
I finish my last cigarette
And go back into the
Mouth of hell for the
Last time with no one
Knowing any different.
It was hot out that day.

keep pouring the salt in

The pain is gone.
Hurt me like the past,
Keep the cut open and
Keep pouring the salt in.
The little things feed me.
Suffering that the
Junkie feels when
There's no fix.
Heartache the date raped
Feel in the shower.
Scrubbing, scrubbing at
Raw flesh that still
Burns with the caress
Of their "love".
Confusion that runs
Through the mind as
Another tries to tell
You of the death of
Parents through tears
And sobs.

Swallow this down your
Mental throat to digest,
A killer rests inside and
The only victim is myself.
I feel your tears,
The pain behind them.
If tears could stop me
I'd never die.

be happy

Passing a woman today
I heard the words 'be happy'.
About the death of grandparents,
And the tyranny of countries?
Loves gone wrong, the weather,
Maybe pets that have met
Their demise under wheels?
Jobs from the past lost?
To a love of words or the
Way a child looks at you
Right after their parents
Have spanked them in the
Middle of a busy department
Store, these empty pockets,
This broken heart, the loss
Of friends or better yet
Stupid people telling perfectly
Fine individuals they don't
Even know to 'be happy'?

If not that then what?

buzzard

There's an angel lying on my bed reading.
I stare at her as I smoke
Wondering if the bastard back at the
Coffee shop is still thinking about her.
She says they're just friends but I've
Never seen friends act like that
Before and when I did they were
In the sack a week later.

He hovered over like a buzzard over prey.
The more I watched the more I
Wanted him to die and the more
I wondered how she would explain it.
But here back in this room I call my
Own it all disappears.
He's not here and the hatred has lessoned.

Jealousy seems to be a mainstay in this
Relationship and a nuisance but we deal.
I get violent towards them and she
Gets bitchy towards the others.
A scary way of showing love,
It works though.
Neither of us forget the other.
It's all from the heart and
This room is too expensive.

rough man

A rough man sits
Smoking his cigarette.
Lives play on his face
Leading to thoughts of
My own past.
Watching him I ponder
My future,
Wondering if it's myself
I see and not him.
Lost in distant ponder,
Myself years from now.
A rough man sitting,
Smoking my cigarette
With someone watching
Pondering their future,
Not wanting to become
A rough man.

The lives play on faces,
Showing the movies
Of one's past.
Silent movies of the
Thirties and all you
Can do is wait for
The words to appear to kill the anticipation
Of a life yet to
Be displayed on the face
Of a rough man smoking
A cigarette.

ego overdose

So many transfer actions
And the dog is still
Running our lives with
Numbers that we don't
Understand or comprehend.
The trumpet will call and
We will all walk with
Nothing but getting there
On our minds.
Truth will show us
Misdeeds of life that
We mistook for good deeds
And we'll all think we're
As righteous as the
Gods themselves.
As we're dying from
Ego overdoses we'll
Realize everything but
Now it's too late,
You're hooked and
There's nothing that
Can save you.

not a career

Sitting in a coffee shop
Noticing my hands were
Red from the scalding
Water that pelts them
Daily for $6.00 an hour.
Taking them away from
The body still lying
In their bed where
They were caressing
It not 20 minutes before.
It's not an intellectual job
But it's a job for now.
Slowly the body will
Deteriorate and be forced
To move on to the
Coffee shop for a cigarette
And a cup of joe,
Mud,
Java,
Black-tea,
Caffeine fix,
And piece of mind.
My lungs hurt also.

New Poems

From past to present our loves shape us
Keeping us held tight against their warmth
Building under us a structure of worth
Constructing around us an assembly of strength
Wrapping the created being in inevitability
Consoling an inner child and preparing eager adults
From loves soft breath our masterpiece emits

constant mask

Circumstances drive you and
The world continues to disappoint.
Look past the masks that
Cover the kingdom.
The shawl of life is something
To occupy the children we are,
Conjoured within minds
Given to us by a maker.
Keep me close and
Realize our insignificance,
Hold tight and let the masks
Take us on our ride.
What happens would have happened
Despite all contortions we try.
To share my mask is
The reason for my mask.
Holding nothing in light but
What has gotten me here.
Remembered.
Forgotten.
Nothing changes what is ahead,
What is ahead changes nothing.
Look to me as I look to you,
For strength and no more.
Going forward is our challenge.
With you I accept it.

regenerative nature of souls

The regenerative nature of our souls
Is what separates us from most.
From the necrotic loss of love
Eating away at those that cling
Too tightly to it once it's gone.
From the hurt brought on by
The heartlessness in this world
Instead of turning forward to
New beginnings and new light.
From the haze brought by
Lies that cloud everything
Including the morals held dear
In a lifetime long left behind.
From the blurring of the line
Separating right from wrong.
Child's ears absorb the meaning
Driven home by the mother's
Hand that follows shortly after.
So clear in the past are most things forgotten.
Words tear down and heal all at once,
Build and destroy with simple utterance.
Where have all the mouths gone now?
Where are the reminders of what
Grounds us to the good inside?
Never having felt it die it must be there,
Hidden away from those that linger
On things in the past or the times
Others would view as dishonorable.
Let the onlookers take the hate
From their own lives and lay it
To rest elsewhere.
Those that reside here know the right,
Feel the wrong, and live with it all.

hot ash

Words poured like hot
Ash from the receiver
As the voice on the other
End began to crack
Under the pressure of
Truth and love's pain.
Finality rushes in as the
First to finish the race
Of emotions that dash
Towards you in mass.
Stepping back from it all,
Giving yourself the
Chance to gather it
Up and analyze the
Reality you begin to
Realize that life has
Brought many obstacles
This only being the latest.
Strength is born of times
Like these and leads
Those caught in the middle
To rise up in support,
Sustenance, love, bravery.
Knowing none of it will
Make a physical difference
Just eases the pain of what
Happens to be for now.
It is things like these that
Offer foundations needed
For the fight that will be
Shared between all as a
Show of power against
That which cannot be seen.

Drawing it all in tight,
Leaving them all closer
In the face of it.

succumb to exploiting

I awoke with the dream
Still lingering along with
The scent of you on me.
Never has a time been
So longed for as the last.

In my slumber I caressed
Every inch of you,
Easing you to the edge
Of creation found only
In whispered moments.
Slowly you raise one then another
Crawling to the middle and
Leaving me chasing after.
Tongues have never melted
As mine did upon your skin,
Tracing you as if heaven
Was ever watchful of the
Treatment of their angels.
Gently your back rose
To my lips and they found you.
I held you there softly
Wanting every minute to
Pass as an hour.
Every lick to feel as if
The earth could swallow us.
Every thrust to bring you
Closer than my skin.
Your hair in my face as
I search for the right spot,
Discovering it hard to find
A wrong one and I
Succumb to exploiting them all.

Wiping the sleep from my eyes
I have found that another day
Awaits without you so the
Night is again longed for,
With dreams keeping us near.

insensitive cold

Softly hold warm embraces
To shield me from the cold
Barrage of the insensitive.
Secrets eroding our true natures.
Tightly grasp my hand
In the open air of morality
As we thumb our noses
Towards its righteous glare.
Let all who ponder realize
That the horror of their
Combined loss is as true
As the nature we hide in.
Warm embraces shielding
Us from the insensitive cold.

unchained whispers

Let secrets free us
From the darkness
Held deep within
As they approach
The proverbial light
Of the mind's day.
Watch as their faces
Draw blank conclusions
While replaying every
Moment over in their minds.
Watch as the realization
Hits them much like
Righteousness strikes
Those that walk the pews.
Watch as the confusion
Turns in them.
Reveals what they've
Always known in their hearts,
That they will never have
This chance that has been
Given this lowly soul.
Hold back the laughter and
Even the tears that you wish
Would ring out and fall for them.
They are the desolate
Canvases of thought
So long awaiting the stroke
From the brush of knowledge
That we have now provided,
Turning once white page
Into the new masterpiece
Of self-taught awareness.
All from the whisper of

Secrets.

perfect shells

Two perfect shells together side by side
Nestled in a pocket safety
Separated only by love's gift.
This one has seen many miles.
It has followed its soul mate's trail.
Searched and explored the world.
Beaten now not by sand and surf,
Beaten now by travel and wear.
A chip hear and crack there,
Tired and weathered by time.
The shell is still perfect
And this shell is mine.
Suspend it above your heart.
Let its love pour over it.
Its perfection pales in
Comparison to yours.

eye of the beholder

Beauty knows no bounds
Once in the beholder's eye.
Physical beauty is a gift
Given to few,
Stifled by many.
True beauty it is said
Exudes from within.
There is no wavering
Of true beauty once seen.
Outer loss of societal
Good looks are trivial.
Hair loss, weight gain,
Acne, scars, cellulite,
Disfiguring accidents
That leave monsters in
Children's eyes have no
Control over what is
Manifested in the mind of
One who looks upon another
With aching heart from the
Swell of love within.
Show me those that speak
Words of sympathy and
Think thoughts of disgust,
I will show you a liar.
Show me love so true it
Blinds the eyes of repulsion,
I will show you a true person.
Leave love to those that
Embrace it entirely.
Bestow condemnation on
Those that fake smiles
With gasps of vulgar reaction.

Hold me as you hold your heart,
With gentle protection.
I will do the same.

muddied transgressions

Forgive us our now muddied
Transgressions that seemed
To begin so innocently.
We tied them down with
The tangled mess we have
Woven through our long
Waits filled with the constant
Yearning that haunts our hours.
It amazes me the amount of
Anticipation that is felt when
Sitting in a seat shared by many
That stands as only mine.
Thousands of miles from you
Yet only hours separate us.
I see the look on your face,
I've seen it for weeks now.
Taunting me with a single
Blow that brings me to my
Knees and wakes me to cold
Sweats and shallow breaths.
I feel your soft whisper
As I draw you close
Grasping you ever tighter
For fear I might lose
You once more to a day,
Week, month, year.
Stay with me and don't
Let your faith falter in the
Face of emotional distress
From times that now leave
You cold and disheartened.
There is no higher being
That will assist us in our

Current plight or offer a
Map to guide the future.
It's left to us and no other.

white knight

Gently hand me
Your fragile heart,
There's a place
That it can heal
And you've yet
To find it within
The madness that
Never ceases here.
Crawl with me
Into a pillowed
Paradise built for
Only you.
Let my arms shield
You from the monster
That haunts your
Every hour.
Allow this knight
To slay the nightmare
You currently find
Yourself in, and never
Doubt his sword is
Yours.

arduous wait

The morning light hits the
Window once again and
A new day starts with
Heavy heart and concern.
It's been far too long.
She'll grow tired of this
Game soon and something
New will catch her eye,
Can't bring myself to blame.
Time heals all wounds and
Yet here it sits taunting the
Both of us and forcefully
Driving a wedge between.
The way is there but hidden,
I'll find it through long search.
My arms will hold her again.
My fingers will trace her
Every outline to create the
Masterpiece in my mind
That could never be put to
Canvas by my own hand.
Do I have to convince her
That it has all been true?
Every word, every passionate
Sigh, or does she cling to it
In hope as I do waiting for
The fateful day of release
When it will all be over and
We can rest together,
Side by weary side.
My breath on the back of
Her neck assuring her I'm there.
Can she wait for the morning

Light to hit the window to
Start a new day with
Weightless heart and
Forgotten concern?
Can she hold out as long
I'm struggling to?

life's nectar

I felt her in the water.
After turning to look
And finding nothing
I realized that most
Every day will be
Filled with moments
That resemble this one.
Again at the bar
The feeling returned.
She was sitting there
In front of me sharing
A drink as if nothing
Was keeping a reality
That has long been
Wished for away.
The feeling returned
When I found myself
Waiting for a glimpse
Of freedom that sits
There preparing one
For a journey that
Needs a jolt, spark,
Push, beginning, start.
She's been here all along.
She watches me when
Everything else is
Pulling the haze of
Life around me.
The sheet of protection
Is continually felt as
I stumble through
This new existence
That is threatening to

Devour everything
I've been working for.
They've bottled it all
For those that wish to
Swallow what is placed
Before them but I can't
Seem to acquire a taste
For the port that's been
Poured in my glass of life.
Walk with me to the water
So I can ensure you'll be
There when I turn around.

keeper of the flame

As sad eyes ponder the smoldering
Coals of a fire stoked far too long
With heartache and mental sweat
You raise them and take in a
Sight you've longed for.
There in your line of vision
Lies a picture perfect fire
Stronger than you could imagine.
Thoughts enter your mind of the
Work that must have been put
Into such a creation, and of
Sorrow for the soul that tends it.
You begin the long journey
To the star-like shimmer
With every step you fight the
Need to look over your shoulder,
Hoping your coals have not
Unexpectedly burst to life.
Knowing a fire so bright could
Sustain you forever you trudge on.
Upon arrival the fire's keeper
Greets you with great smiles and
Comfort you've longed for.
Examining this being you begin
To realize there are no signs of
Hard labor or tearful strain.
He answers your stares with elation.
This fire was but only coals
Not too long ago.
As I sat in despair over the end,
Exhausted from my fight,
Growing colder with every breath
The coals began to awaken.

With no effort or pain the flames
Grew stronger than before,
Leaving me warmed and calmed.
Looking to the outside world
For answers or causes there was
Only you on the horizon traveling
Towards my newfound light.
I've watched you for days.
Watched the tiny speck grow to
Have a form in the distance.
The closer you drew the stronger
The fire became and the more
Comforted I began to feel.
Would you share this warmth
That you've brought me or
Are your travels taking you on?
I fear if you continue this new
Life will dwindle to smoldering
Coals and my work will begin again.
If you wish to stay I promise to
Keep this blaze as sturdy as
You see before you now.
You will never have to labor at it.
You will never have to worry.
You will never have to wipe the
Sweat from your brow.
You will only have to be here,
I will take care of the rest.

reassuring hand

Slide your hand around
Mine and squeeze.
Feel what you want,
Want what you need.
Consent to the
Happiness that awaits you.
Follow as I guide you to it.
Inconsistencies of life
Will never end.
Let us lay embrace
Where embrace need laid.
Look to the future and
Trust that the path
Is where you want to be.
Permit my final wish
To take you from here.
From the present and past,
From pain and injury,
From loveless hearts,
From densely lit flames
Of intellect that destroy
You as they fade further
Into the darkness of hate.
Intertwine our fingers
As the horizon grows
For only us.
Presenting the one thing
Needed by us both;
Light.

bumpy ride

Too many things have
Muddied the water we
Tread and the last thing
We need is the storm
Approaching from the west.
Tightly strap yourself in.
Rides this bumpy are rarely
Survived, but I have faith.
Black horizons can't batter
The bow of vessels such as
This enough to invite sinking.
We may come out the other
Side bruised and bandaged.
Can you withstand the
Physical pain with me as
We heal together?

other side of morning

As the awakening of a
New cherished dawn
Approaches on the horizon
Of our dreamscape
We begin to realize the
Destitute we have
Brought upon our
Souls and we revel in it.
Soaking like soft infants
In the glory of all
We have assembled in
The light for one great
Triumphant coup of hearts.
Ours are the unbreakable.
We have given ourselves
To endless possibilities,
From those of grandeur and
Shared solitude to the feared
Nightmares of star-crossed
Never to become one
In the multitude of pairings.
We will take it all and
Fail at nothing.
As dusk envelopes the
Vessel that brought us
This far we fall into what
Could be the end,
Sparking our beginning.

Your scent lingers on me
Through the depths of dreams.
The only thing carrying
Me to the other side of morning.

trivial distance

Hold tight to the realization
That what we have spans
Mountains, deserts, plains and
The unimaginable indifference
That has pulled us through
The years we've lost in
Situations we had all but
Prayed for yet now find
Ourselves trapped in.
Look up from the floor of
Your mental dungeon and
You'll see it small as it is.
You know immediately
It's there staring back at you,
The tiny speck of light
Making you realize there
Is a way out and you've
Found it by mistake.
Fate has played its hand
For both of us and
I'm all in standing at the top
Waiting for you to break through
To the other side of an
Existence we know is there
But have only found in
Sacrosanct moments stolen
From the daft world that
Surrounds us daily.
Reach for my hand
It hasn't been an illusion
For some time now.

positive outlook of the future

The week begins again and
My heart leaps from slumber
Long before my mind.
It will be just four short hours
Until that voice is heard once more.
The voice that caused such
Sorrow only days before
As it whispered goodbye,
Followed by I love you.
The start of the week brings
New tales of heartache and smiles
That lead to deep discussion and
Soft laughter that fills the ego.
Deep thought that confirms the love.
She says she's sorry again and again.
Always baffled me that people feel
Sorry for things that have brought
Them so much joy and so often
Bring with them some form of
Drawback or disillusioned perfection.
Everything has a dark side or
Unforeseen downside that if you
Could experience prior to the
Enjoyment it might have righted
Your thinking in some fashion.
Too many things in life could be
Left unimagined if this philosophy
Took hold of the race and directed it.
Given the choice I would much
Rather have had the joy and dealt
With the rest than never
Have lived at all.
Knowing the consequences and

Gambling against them drives the
Week's morning-beginning much
Further than the dread of never
Having a light until the end of the tunnel.
The soft laughs and deep discussion
Will continue to drive me through
The days without,
Until the days are through.

escape it all

If the eternal question
Were posed would you
Smile upon the endlessly
Broken promise of infinite
Happiness laid before you?
Turning a tear-stained
Cheek to the periodic joy
We find ourselves lost in
Would the I do ring
Forever in my ears
Deafening the laughter I
Once evoked from you?
Would the star-crossed
Time we spent melt
Away into the wretched
Reality we force ourselves
Through to get to the next
Moment together?
Would the clock stop
Ticking away the minutes
That draw you closer?
Would I be stuck with
The decision of freedom
With nothing to enjoy freely
Or would the cheek turn
In this direction with numbing
Reassurance that nothing
Will change in the only sane
Corner of life I enjoy spending
The free moments
So profoundly cherished?
Would your eyes swell
With tears of comfort

For an unbeating heart
Bringing it back to life
With a single gasp?
Would your consoling
Caress lead to the all
Too often awaited release
We both treasure?
Would your answer make
Decisions heavily weighed
Exulted and worthwhile?
Would you run with me?

tedious moments

Let not the absence
Grow the heart fonder.
Let the missed moments
Of bliss stolen during
Long distant hours
Provide the clarity of
Reason and emotion
That are presently driving
Us through the storm.
Let not the ever present
Cause of harsh feelings
Sour gentle souls.
Let the return of constant
Caresses guide us through
The downpour of confusion.
Embrace the dawn that
Rests on the far off horizon,
Calculate the miles, and
Begin the journey with one step.
Estimate the distance and
Dream it to inches.
Determine the outcome and
Live the tedious moments
That keep you from it.
Be thankful we've found
A new path,
However rocky the present
Terrain may appear.

4:42 am

Drinking coffee at 4:42 am.
Sleep broken by a crying feline
More than likely a lack of food
But on this night it seemed
Urgent enough to begin at 2:00.
Finally rising I check a full bowl,
The dog in the back yard, and
Nothing out of place enough to
Warrant the alarm she sounded.
So softly sipping I ponder at 4:42 am.
The quiet reflection at this hour deafening.
Eight months from now a new
Child will sound alarms in
Varying degrees of discomfort:
Want, need, fear, loneliness.
Shifts will be dealt and we'll
Both clamber to take them,
Each wanting every new moment
With our child with no regard for sleep.
Each holding, rocking, lulling
Back to an awkward slumber
This being that now breaths our air,
As the other watches with
Filled heart and renewed life.
The tender care only mothers
Possess showered upon this life.
Its bed will be her arms,
My eyes its ever present protection.
Our love will pour from us
In constant flows of worry and want.
Worry of the things we
Cannot keep from it.
Want of the things

We hope to provide.
In these sleepless hours
We'll be three alone,
Intertwined arms of lullaby
Our heartbeats the only melody.
I picture it in fantasy.
Knowing that a reality awaits me
Of afternoon naps overflowing
With our combined emotions as
We watch, silently holding each
Other in amazement of what
Our love has created.
But for now coffee's quiet
Reflection rules 4:42 am.

she's finally here

When I look into her eyes
I want to shout to the heavens
And stomp on hell's ceiling
Letting them know that my
Beautiful mate has given
Birth to their new ruler,
Their queen, their goddess.
I hope they're ready for her.
I've been waiting a long time.

toxic disregard

Industry is feeding us toxic disregard
While the corporations tell our government
What to say to calm us.
Keeping us frightened enough not
To question the logic but
Not frightened enough to stop purchasing.
The new hope and change
Has now awakened on Jan 21st
To the stark reality of control,
Who has it and who can use it.
Amazing how well the puppets
Perform in the nickel show
When you're willing to pay a dollar.

other's words

Lost in a sea of
Red satin and other's words.
The feral feline
Stretches out to lay
Its tiny paw on your
Shoulder while cackling.
You reached the
End of your wits and
Solitude shared with
Profound words has
Become your only escape.
Your own would once suffice
But then what was once
Yours remained that way,
Only being shared if you
Felt the inspired need.
The lock is now broken
On the safe that formerly
Protected both your
Mind and soul spilled
On crystal paper.
So many of them
Have been lost in the
Subservient subconscious
That you once trusted.
Running through mental
Forests you've been damned
To find concealed spaces
To bury these previously
Protected slivers of expression.
But for now the feral feline
Comforts you as if it knows
You're drowning in sea of

Red satin and other's words.

Brandon Ogle was born May 1978 in Springfield, Missouri to an automobile interior designing father and a Jane of all trades mother. He began writing at the age of 15 with his prose featured in small trade magazines and collaborative compositions. The nomadic life he lived through corporate success found in the technology industry left his writing dormant for nearly 10 years.

The author's works focus on the mundane existence that we all find ourselves enduring and the inevitable lessons learned through persevering those moments. Each word inviting you into those times to share the retrospect of similar experience. Welcoming you to your world, shared by so many and told in these works.

> As the body of works grows
> So too does the mind and soul.

www.ingramcontent.com/pod-product-compliance
Lightning Source LLC
Chambersburg PA
CBHW021947290426
44108CB00012B/980